The Little Book
of
Spiritual Wisdom

by Dr. Morris Gall

Compiled by: Dr. Morris Gall
Cover Illustration by: Laura Bruzzese
Cover Design by: Bostrom Publishing
Typeset and Design by: Julie Otlewis

Published by Great Quotations Publishing Company
1967 Quincy Court
Glendale Heights, Illinois 60139

Printed in Hong Kong

We live in a pluralism of religious convictions. Even if your beliefs are absolute, you cannot force them on others. You can only try to understand them. Familiarity with the spiritual wisdom of other faiths can enlarge your outlook and bring you closer to your global neighbors. You will see through the passages in this book, how humanity is similar in its quest for ultimate values though expressions and ways of this search may be different.

Dr. Morris Gall is most suitable for compiling this variety of scriptural verses. With a Judeo-Christian background, he has lived in Japan, where he encountered the Chinese, Hindu, and Buddhist religious milieu.

It is real joy for me to present this jewelry box of timeless spiritual wisdom.

Nobuo Kobayashi
Professor Emeritus, School of Theology,
Kwansei Gakuin University,
Nishinomiya, Japan

I command enjoyment, for there is nothing better for people under the sun than to eat, and drink and enjoy themselves.

— Old Testament

God stands by those who act kindly.

— The Koran

Let us live happily then, free from greed
among the greedy!

— Buddhism

God loves people who love to give.

— New Testament

The cultured are so fond of learning that they are not ashamed to pick up knowledge even from their inferiors.

— Confucianism

Do not let ill-will toward any folk incriminate you so that you swerve from dealing justly.

— The Koran

You shall not spread a false report.

— Old Testament

Let no one forget his own good for the sake of another's, however great; let a man, after he has discerned what his good is, be ever intent upon it.

— Buddhism

**Visit solitary places
and stay a while.
Do not delight in crowds.**

— Hinduism

Cooperate with one another for virtue and heedfulness, and do not cooperate with one another for the purpose of vice and aggression.

— The Koran

If you put yourself above others, you will be put down. But if you humble yourself, you will be honored.

— New Testament

To see what is right and not do it,
is cowardice.

— Confucianism

Men without delusions have overcome the
damage done by attachments. Desire has
dwindled away. From opposites as we know
them -- joy, grief -- They are set free.

— Hinduism

Better to stop in time than to fill to
  overflowing.
Oversharpen a blade and the edge will
  weaken.
Fill the house with gold and jade but none can
  preserve them.
Amass wealth and awards with pride and they
  will attract disaster.
Withdraw when the work is done. Such is the
  way of Heaven.

— Taoism

Gentle thoughts bring happiness.

— Old Testament

If some scoundrel should come up to you with some piece of news, clear up the facts lest you afflict some folk out of ignorance.

— The Koran

The Master's manner was affable yet firm, commanding but not harsh, polite but easy.

— Confucianism

The fields are damaged by weeds, mankind is damaged by hatred: Therefore a gift bestowed on those who do not hate brings great rewards.

— Buddhism

Wisdom is better than weapons of war.

— Old Testament

You obey the law of Christ when you offer each other a helping hand.

— New Testament

Man should not give up work natural to him even though it is imperfect; imperfection mars all undertakings as smoke clouds the fire.

— Hinduism

There is no curse like covetousness.
He who knows what is enough will always
have enough.

— Taoism

High office filled by people of narrow views
I cannot bear to see.

— Confucianism

No one remains inactive even for a moment.
The state of all existence makes everyone act
in spite of himself.

— Hinduism

Do everything properly and in order.

— New Testament

Do not let one set of people make fun of
another set, nor let any women mistreat other
women. Nor should you criticize one another
nor insult one another by using nicknames.

— The Koran

If a person does not trust, others will not
trust him.

— Taoism

The right material is hard to find.

— Confucianism

Riches destroy the foolish if they look not for
the other shore; by his thirst for riches the
foolish man destroys himself as if he were his
own enemy.

— Buddhism

Do not give short measures and weight . . .
and do not cheat men of their belongings nor
cause havoc on earth as mischief makers.

— The Koran

God will bless you, if you have to suffer for
doing something good.

— New Testament

Overcome anger by mildness; overcome evil by good; overcome the miser by liberality, the liar by truth!

— Buddhism

It is true that the world is enslaved by activity but the exception is work for the sake of sacrifice.

— Hinduism

A good word may be compared to a good tree whose root is firm and whose branches soar up into the sky.

— The Koran

When the ruler regulates lightly the people are simple and relaxed. When the ruler regulates harshly the people are wily and restless.

— Taoism

Let there be no strife between you and me for we are kindred.

— Old Testament

The world our senses touch is hot or cold,
pleasant or unpleasant. Sensations come and
go. They do not last. Learn to endure them.

— Hinduism

As the jasmine sheds its withered flowers,
even so, men should shed lust and hatred.

— Buddhism

Attack the evil that is within yourself; do not attack the evil that is in others.

— Confucianism

Anyone who commits evil or harms himself, then seeks forgiveness from God, will find God is forgiving, merciful.

— The Koran

The way you treat others is the way you will
be treated.

— New Testament

He who is good does not have much. He who
has much is not good.

— Taoism

Just as the ether, present everywhere, is too subtle to be polluted by anything, the self, though pervading the whole body, is not polluted.

— Hinduism

No one should separate a couple that God has joined together.

—New Testament

Wrongdoers will not prosper.

— The Koran

An evil deed is best left undone, for one feels remorse for it afterwards; a good deed is better done, for having done it, one does not feel remorse.

— Buddhism

The Master was asked, Is there any single saying that one can act upon all day and everyday? He replied, "Perhaps the saying about consideration: Never do to others what you would not like them to do to you."

— Confucianism

Exalt not excellence and people will not contend. Prize not possessions and people will not steal. Display not the desirable and people will not be disturbed.

— Taoism

Whatever your hand finds to do, do it with your might.

— Old Testament

If a man has the habit of reverence and ever respects the aged, four things will increase for him: life, beauty, happiness, power.

— Buddhism

In old days people studied for the sake of self-improvement; nowadays they study in order to impress other people.

— Confucianism

Do not indulge in shocking acts which you may practice either openly or kept secret.

— The Koran

Bravado when strong hastens decay. This is contrary to TAO. What is contrary to TAO comes to an early end.

— Taoism

The Lord: I love the man of devotion. He is
equal-minded to friend and foe, to honor and
shame, heat and cold, to pleasant and
unpleasant things. He is equally unaffected by
praise and blame, is content with whatever
comes his way.

— Hinduism

Be sensible and don't tell everything you know.

— Old Testament

If a traveller does not meet with one who is better or his equal, let him keep firmly to his solitary journey; there is no companionship with a fool.

— Buddhism

One whose heart is in the smallest degree set
upon goodness will dislike no one.

— Confucianism

Liquor and gambling, idols and raffles, are only
the filthy work of Satan; turn aside from it so
that you may prosper.

— The Koran

In speech, be true. In ruling, preserve order.
In business, show facility. In action, be timely.

— Taoism

As a bee collects nectar and departs without
injuring the flower or its colour or scent, so let
a sage go about a village.

— Buddhism

**You know that many runners enter a race, and only one of them wins the prize.
So run to win!**

— New Testament

A good person covets the reputation of being slow in word but prompt in deed.

— Confucianism

Whatever I did improperly to you, jokingly in playing, resting, sitting or eating, either by myself or in public -- Oh imperishable Lord, I ask your pardon for it.

— Hinduism

Powerful weapons are portents of woe.
They are despised by the well bred.
A man of TAO shuns them.

— Taoism

Stay away from stupid and senseless
arguments. They only lead to trouble.

— New Testament

Do not worry over something you have no knowledge about.

— The Koran

The fault of others is easily perceived, but that of one's self is difficult to perceive.

— Buddhism

If you find you have made a mistake, you must not be afraid of admitting the fact and amending your ways.

— Confucianism

Please, God, be patient with me as a father with his son, a friend with his friend, a lover with his beloved.

— Hinduism

Put up with each other, and forgive anyone
who does you wrong.

— New Testament

If a man speaks or acts with a pure thought,
happiness follows him, like a shadow that
never leaves him.

— Buddhism

It is only the very wisest and the very stupidest who cannot change.

— Confucianism

If the light of a thousand suns should effulge all at once, it would resemble the radiance of the God of overpowering reality.

— Hinduism

One's own self conquered is better than the conquest of all other people.

— Buddhism

One who has given up all desire and moves about without wanting anything. Who says neither mine nor I wins peace.

— Hinduism

He who is brave in daring will be killed. He who is brave in not daring will survive.

— Taoism

It's stupid to say bad things about your
neighbors. If you are sensible,
you will keep quiet.

— Old Testament

Do not spoil things on earth once they have
been improved.

— The Koran

He who is courteous is not scorned; he who is of good faith is trusted by the people; he who is diligent succeeds in all he undertakes.

— Confucianism

Irrigators guide the water (wherever they like); fletchers bend the arrow; carpenters bend a log of wood; good people fashion themselves.

— Buddhism

The best soldiers show no rashness.
The best fighters display no anger.
The best conqueror seeks no revenge.
The best employer serves those
he employs.

— Taoism

Do not act as an advocate for traitors.

— The Koran

In the body restraint is good, good is restraint in speech; in thought restraint is good, good is restraint in all things. A mouth restrained in all things is freed from suffering.

— Buddhism

Keep away from worthless and useless talk.

— New Testament

Kind words are like honey. They cheer you up and make you feel strong.

— Old Testament

He who is self-assertive has no merit.

— Taoism

Maids and valets are very hard to deal with.
If you are friendly with them they get out of
hand, and if you keep your distance they
resent it.

— Confucianism

He who promises lightly is of little faith.

— Taoism

Pollution has appeared on land and at sea because of what man's hands have accomplished, so He may let them taste something of what they have earned, in order that they will turn back in repentance.

— The Koran

The mind and will is difficult to control and fickle. But by training and ascetic practice it is possible to control it.

— Hinduism

Whenever you judge between people, you should judge with justice.

— The Koran

Make up your mind not to upset anyone's faith.

— New Testament

It is good to tame the mind, which is difficult to hold in and flighty, rushing wherever it tilts; a tamed mind brings happiness.

— Buddhism

A good man is ashamed to let his words outrun his deeds.

— Confucianism

God does not love someone who is conceited, boastful, nor those who are tight-fisted and order other people to be stingy.

— The Koran

Too much pride brings disgrace; humility leads to honor.

— Old Testament

Whoever is born will die, and whoever dies will certainly be born. Since this cannot be changed, your grief is inappropriate.

— Hinduism

You may rob the army of its commander-in-chief, but you cannot deprive the humblest peasant of his opinion.

— Confucianism

It is better to live alone, there is no companionship with a fool; let a man walk alone, let him commit no sin, let him do with few wishes, like an elephant in the forest.

— Buddhism

A tree as large as a man's embrace springs
from a tiny sprout.

— Taoism

Fight those who fight against you...
yet do not initiate hostilities; God does not
love aggressors.

— The Koran

Clever talk and pretentious manners are
seldom found in a good person.

— Confucianism

If you have food, share it with someone else.

— New Testament

The Lord is present inside all beings, moving all of them like puppets by his magic power.

— Hinduism

Love of courage without love of learning degenerates into mere recklessness.

— Confucianism

Do not speak harshly to anybody; those who are spoken to will answer you in the same way. Angry speech breeds trouble; you will receive blow for blow.

— Buddhism

Agitation over anything spoils it. Grasping means losing.

— Taoism

**Don't brag about tomorrow!
Each day brings its own surprises.**

— Old Testament

Endure patiently whatever may afflict you...
Act modestly in the way you walk, and lower
your voice.

— The Koran

No one sees the beginning of things but only
the middle. Their end also is unseen.
There is no reason to lament.

— Hinduism

Doing what is right and fair pleases the Lord more than an offering.

— Old Testament

Ask and you will receive. Search, and you will find. Knock, and the door will be opened to you.

— New Testament

In friendship repeated scolding can only lead to estrangement.

— Confucianism

Do not have evildoers for friends, do not have low people for friends; have virtuous people for friends, have for friends the best of men.

— Buddhism

Love is always supportive, loyal, hopeful, and trusting.

– New Testament

That person is disciplined and happy who can prevail over the turmoil that springs from desire and anger here on earth.

— Hinduism

Heavy drinkers and those who live only for pleasure will lose all they have.

— Old Testament

There is no fire like lust; there is no losing throw like hatred; there is no pain like this body; there is no happiness higher than peace.

— Buddhism

The Master said Yen P'ing Chung was a good example of what one's relationship with others should be. However long he has known anyone he always maintains the same scrupulous courtesy.

— Confucianism

When you judge others, you condemn
yourself.

— New Testament

Few learn the lessons of silence. Few seek the
fruit of non-action.

– Taoism

When you know a thing, to recognize that you know it, and when you do not know a thing, to recognize that you do not know it — that is knowledge.

— Confucianism

Never does hatred cease by hatred here below: hatred ceases by love; this is an eternal law.

— Buddhism

Win the world by letting alone.
The more taboos and inhibitions in the world
The poorer the people become.
The more law and order is trumpeted
The more robbers and thieves thrive.

— Taoism

If you won't help the poor, don't expect to be heard when you cry out for help.

— Old Testament

To know you do not know is insight. To think you know when you do not is sickness.

— Taoism

God does not harm mankind in any way but men do harm themselves.

— The Koran

The business of the teacher is to give fresh life to the Scriptures by reinterpreting them so that they apply to the problems of modern life.

— Confucianism

When a man allows his mind to obey the whims of his senses, it destroys his judgement like a storm destroys a ship.

— Hinduism

All that the Law says can be summed up in the command to love others as much as you love yourself.

— New Testament

A day with your Lord is like a thousand years such as you count by.

— The Koran

If a man is engaged in his proper work he
attains the highest end.

— Hinduism

Any thought of accepting wealth and rank by
means that I know to be wrong is as remote
from me as the clouds that float above.

— Confucianism

**The tranquil is master of
the turbulent.
To be rash is to lose control.**

— Taoism

To go too far is as bad as not to go far enough.

— Confucianism

Every nation has its term; so whenever their deadline comes, they will not postpone it for an hour, nor will they advance it.

— The Koran

When people ask you for something,
give it to them.

— New Testament

He who possesses character and
discrimination, who is just, speaks the truth,
and does what is his own business, him the
world will hold dear.

— Buddhism

Do not argue with the People of the Book unless it is in the politest manner...
Our God and your God is the same One.

— The Koran

Awake and sing for joy!

— Old Testament

Let a wise man blow away his own impurities
as a smith blows away the impurities of silver,
one by one, little by little, and from instant to
instant.

— Buddhism

What is this worldly life except an amusement and a game?

— The Koran

He who acts demonstrates integrity when he is freed from attachments, does not speak of himself, is steady and energetic, and is not changed by success or failure.

— Hinduism

A good person reverences those that excel but tolerates all; he commends the good and empathizes with the incapable.

— Confucianism

He who stands on tiptoe is not steady.
He who swaggers will stumble.

— Taoism

As a solid rock is not shaken by the wind, wise people falter not amidst blame and praise.

— Buddhism

You shall serve God alone, and treat your parents kindly, and also near relatives, orphans and the needy, and say kind things to other people, and keep up prayer and pay the welfare tax.

— The Koran

Seek distraction in the arts.

— Confucianism

Give up trying so hard to get rich. Your
money flies away before you know it, just like
an eagle suddenly taking off.

— Old Testament

Great talents ripen slowly.

— Taoism

When peacemakers plant seeds of peace they will harvest justice.

— New Testament

With the disruption of the family, the eternal family tradition perishes. With the collapse of tradition, chaos overtakes the whole race. Chaos leads to the corruption of women in the family. When the women are corrupted the whole society erodes.

— Hinduism

Health is the greatest of blessings,
contentedness the best riches; trust is the best
of relationships, Nirvana the highest happiness.

— Buddhism

You will know the truth, and the truth will set
you free.

— New Testament

The fields are weedy and wild.
The granaries are empty.
To be decked in finery, filled with food and
drink, owning too much wealth.
This is riotous brigandage.
All too far from the TAO.

— Taoism

Do not cause havoc on earth like mischief makers.

— The Koran

The good man calls attention to the good points in others; he does not call attention to their defects. The small man does just the reverse of this.

— Confucianism

If you sleep all the time, you will starve; if you get up and work, you will have enough food.

— Old Testament

Practice equanimity always, whether luck grants your wishes or not.

— Hinduism

Pleasant is virtue lasting to old age; pleasant is a faith firmly rooted; pleasant is the attainment of intelligence; pleasant is the avoidance of sins.

— Buddhism

If you counsel a ruler entreat him to desist in dominating the world by force. Adoption of force is apt to rebound.

— Taoism

To be poor and not resent it is far harder than to be rich, yet not presumptuous.

– Confucianism

Store up your treasures in heaven where moths and rust cannot destroy them, and thieves cannot break in and steal them!

— New Testament

The Lord: Of every world brought forth I am beginning, middle and end. I am the knowledge that affects the self, the true subject of learned debaters.

— Hinduism

Amend your ways and your doings.

— Old Testament

Brambles grow where armies gather.
Great battles are followed by lean harvests.
The wise do only what needs to be done.
And never strive to subdue the world.

— Confucianism

The Master spoke of low-down creatures. Before they have got office, they think about nothing but how to get it; when they have it all they care about is to avoid losing it; so soon as they see themselves in the slightest danger of losing it, there is no length to which they will not go.

— Confucianism

How can you teach others when you refuse
to learn?

— New Testament

From the fruit of the datepalm and grapevine
you derive intoxicants as well as fine
nourishment; in that is a sign for folk
who reason.

— The Koran

Three treasures I cherish:
The first is fathomless love,
The second is frugality,
The third is reluctance to lead.
From love comes courage,
From frugality generosity,
From reticence comes leadership.

— Taoism

He who trusts in his spiritual guides gains understanding . . . Having gained understanding he soon reaches supreme peace. The man full of doubts has neither this world nor the next for happiness.

— Hinduism

The fate of humans and the fate of animals is the same; as one dies, so dies the other. They all have the same breath, and humans have no advantage over the animals.

— Old Testament

Eat wholesome things and act honorably.

— The Koran

One who will not worry about what is far off
will soon find something worse than worry
close at hand.

— Confucianism

There is no greatness like the greatness of Heaven.

— Confucianism

More blessings come from giving than from receiving.

— New Testament

Follow whatever has been inspired in you and be patient.

— The Koran

Cheat the poor to make profit or give gifts to the rich -- either way you lose.

— Old Testament

Parents, don't be hard on your children.

— New Testament

Patiently shall I endure abuse as the elephant
in battle endures the arrow sent from the bow:
for the world is ill-natured.

— Buddhism

Show kindness to your parents. Never scold
either of them. Speak to them in a generous
fashion. Protect them carefully from outsiders.

— The Koran

When a bird is about to die its song touches the heart. When a man is about to die his words are of note.

— Confucianism

There is a time for surging ahead and a time
for staying behind.
A time for breathing softly and a time for
breathing strongly.
A time for vigor and a time for withdrawal.
A time for soaring upward and a time for
lying low.
Thus the sage shuns excess, extremes
and smugness.

— Taoism

What makes man do wrong even without
wanting to?
The Lord: It is desire, and anger.

— Hinduism

Losing self-control leaves you as helpless as a
city without a wall.

— Old Testament

Anything you have is temporary; while
whatever God has is everlasting.

— The Koran

When the Master was asked about goodness
he said: in private life, courteous, in public life
diligent, in relationships, loyal.

— Confucianism

You cannot pick figs or grapes from
thorn bushes.

— New Testament

To venture with love is to win the battle.
To defend with love is to be invulnerable.
Heaven saves and guards with love.

— Taoism

A good man obtains the confidence of those under him before putting burdens upon them; and the confidence of those above him before criticizing them.

— Confucianism

Man should discover his own reality and not thwart himself. For he has the self as his friend or as his only enemy.

— Hinduism

Do not squander money extravagantly.

— The Koran

If by leaving a small pleasure one sees a great
pleasure, let a wise man leave the small
pleasure and look to the great.

— Buddhism

When others are happy, be happy with them, and when they are sad, be sad.

— New Testament

When the Master was very ill and a disciple asked leave to perform the Rite of Expiation, the Master said: "...what justifies me in the eyes of Heaven is the life 1 have led."

— Confucianism

No burdened soul may bear another's burden.

— The Koran

That a person strays from the path is no reason
for rejection. Did the ancients not declare:
He who seeks finds. He who has faults
is forgiven.

—Taoism

If you have good sense, instruction will help you have even better sense.

— Old Testament

Just as a man discards worn-out clothes and puts on others that are new, the embodied leaves behind worn-out bodies and enters new ones.

— Hinduism

Forget those things that are behind, reaching forward to the things in the future.

— New Testament

You shall not tattoo any marks upon you.

— Old Testament

Be careful about what you say. For a single word you may be set down as wise, for a single word you may be set down as a fool.

— Confucianism

All tremble at punishment, all fear death; remembering that you are like them, do not strike or slay.

— Buddhism

Do your work willingly, as though you were serving the Lord himself, and not just your earthly master.

— New Testament

**In dwelling, cherish the ground.
In meditating, go deep in
the heart.
In dealing with others,
be genial and kind.**

— Taoism

Do not act afraid; you will come out on top.

— The Koran

To speak without irritating others, words that are true, pleasing, and beneficial ...that is austerity in speech.

— Hinduism

Silently search your heart as you lie in bed.

— Old Testament

The Master said: I have never yet seen anyone whose desire to build up his moral power was as strong as sexual desire.

— Confucianism

Don't fall in love with money. Be satisfied
with what you have.

— New Testament

The soft and weak overcome the strong and
hard. Yielding is the method of TAO.

— Taoism

One whose misdeeds are covered with good deeds, brightens up the world, like the moon when freed from clouds.

— Buddhism

One who knows does not tell.
One who tells does not know.

— Taoism

The Lord:
When you offer with love a leaf,
a flower, or water to me I accept
that offer of love from the giver
who gives himself.

— Hinduism

The Master fished with a line but not with a net; when fowling he did not aim at a roosting bird.

— Confucianism

They will not have any idle talk there [in Paradise] nor any faultfinding, merely people saying, "Peace! Peace!"

— The Koran

A foolish person is one who does not let go of sleep, fear, sorrow, despondency, and pride.

— Hinduism

If you want too much and are too lazy to work, it could be fatal.

— Old Testament

Act before there is a problem. Bring order
before there is disorder.

— Taoism

The man who gives himself to drinking
intoxicating liquors in this world, digs up his
own roots.

— Buddhism

If any means of escaping poverty presented
itself, that did not involve doing wrong,
I would adopt it even though my employment
were the most menial.

— Confucianism

Eat any lawful wholesome thing . . . God has
only forbidden you carrion, blood, and pork.

— The Koran

When you pray, don't talk on and on. Your
Father knows what you need before you ask.

— New Testament

Great accomplishments are possible with
attention to small beginnings.

— Taoism

He who holds back rising anger like a rolling chariot, him I call a real driver; other people are but holding the reins.

— Buddhism

You shall not follow a majority in
doing wrong.

— Old Testament

The Master said, "My disciple was not any help
to me; he accepted everything I said."

— Confucianism

The wise man submits to my grace at the end of many births. He realizes: God is all. This exalted person is exceptional.

— Hinduism

Do not break any oaths once they have been sworn.

— The Koran

God bless those people who are humble.
The earth will belong to them!

— New Testament

Rulers who regulate through artifice are
malefactors of the realm. Rulers who cast
aside craft are benefactors of the realm.

— Taoism

When the Master was asked about government
he said: do not try to hurry things.
Ignore minor considerations.

— Confucianism

I take refuge with the Lord from the evil of the
stealthy whisperer.

— The Koran

Humility is the root of greatness.

— Taoism

Bad deeds and deeds that are harmful to ourselves are easy to do; what is salutary and good, that is very difficult to do.

— Buddhism

In dealing with the aged, comfort them; in dealing with friends, be of good faith with them; in dealing with the young, cherish them.

— Confucianism

Be sure you have sound advice before making plans or starting a war.

— Old Testament

That person existing in everyone's body is forever inviolable. Therefore you should not sorrow for any creatures.

— Hinduism

Him indeed I call a Brahmin who is tolerant with the intolerant, mild among the violent, and free from greed among the greedy.

— Buddhism

The greatest carver does the least cutting.

— Taoism

Do not prance saucily around the earth.

— The Koran

God will be as hard on you as you are on others! He will treat you exactly as you treat them.

— New Testament

The Master said, when everyone dislikes a man, enquiry is necessary; when everyone likes a man, enquiry is necessary.

— Confucianism

Show patience. God stands beside the patient.

— The Koran

Knowing others is wisdom. Knowing oneself
is enlightenment.

— Taoism

Every day I examine myself on these points: in
acting on behalf of others have I always been
loyal to their interests? Have I always been
true to my word?

— Confucianism

A gossip tells everything, but a true friend will keep a secret.

— Old Testament

Victory breeds hatred, for the conquered is unhappy. One who has given up both victory and defeat, the contented, is happy.

— Buddhism

Anyone who spares life acts as if he had granted life to all mankind.

— The Koran

A gusty wind cannot last all morning.
A sudden downpour cannot last all day.
Even Heaven and Earth cannot make
things eternal.
Much less can man.

— Taoism

A gift is a gift of integrity when it is given at the right time to the proper person, to one who cannot be expected to return the gift - and given merely because it should be given.

— Hinduism

Do not spy on one another nor let any of you backbite others.

— The Koran

One who seeks only coarse food to eat, water to drink and bent arm for pillow, will without looking for it find happiness to boot.

— Confucianism

If an occasion arises friends are pleasant;
enjoyment is pleasant when one shares it with
another; a good work is pleasant in the hour of
death; the giving up of all grief is pleasant.

— Buddhism

Your heart will always be where your
treasure is.

— New Testament

He whom others fear, likewise cannot but fear others.

— Taoism

If a person has wonderful gifts yet is arrogant and mean, all the rest is of no account.

— Confucianism

Practice forgiveness, command decency; and avoid ignorant people.

— The Koran

A man is not learned because he talks much; he who is patient, free from hatred and fear, he is called learned.

— Buddhism

Wisdom is shown to be right by what it does.

— New Testament

There is no greater misery than misjudging the foe. To make light of the foe is to lose one's treasure.

— Taoism

Let not the wise boast in their wisdom; let not the mighty boast in their might; let not the wealthy boast in their wealth.

— Old Testament

The orphan must not be exploited and the beggar should not be brushed aside.

— The Koran

Any men, save those who are truly good, if their sufferings are very great, will be likely to rebel.

— Confucianism

The Lord: Demonic people do not comprehend religious acts or search for release. They have criminal aspirations to amass money for the indulgence of their desires. These people, so full of scorn, rely on their egos, on force, on pride, on lust and wrath; and they hate me.

— Hinduism

Excessive attainment will prove expensive;
Hoarding goods will lead to heavy loss;
A contented man is immune
to disappointment.
To know when to stop is to avoid danger.

— Taoism

Money wrongly gotten will disappear bit by bit; money earned little by little will grow and grow.

— Old Testament

The Lord does not love those who are aggressive.

— The Koran

**The gates of hell destroying
the soul are threefold:
desire, anger, and greed.
Therefore these three
should be avoided.**

— Hinduism

People often fail on the verge of victory.
With watchfulness at the start, and patience
at the end, nothing will be undone.

— Taoism

Children are not supposed to save up for their
parents, but parents are supposed to take care
of their children.

— New Testament

A good person takes as much trouble to discover what is right as lesser ones take to discern what will pay.

— Confucianism

It's smart to be patient, but it's stupid to lose your temper.

— Old Testament

Do not shout in your prayer nor say it under your breath; seek a course in between.

— The Koran

Never give up!

— New Testament

A violent person will meet a violent end.

— Taoism

Man is qualified for reaching the Divine when no longer centered in his ego, freed from reliance on force; from pride, desire, anger, attachment to possessions; when he is unselfish, at peace.

— Hinduism

Respect the young. How do you know that they will not one day be all that you are now?

— Confucianism

In quietness and in trust shall be your strength.

— Old Testament

The world is a sacred vessel which none should injure. One who tampers with it spoils it. One who grasps it loses it.

— Taoism

In vain I have looked for a single man capable of seeing his own faults and bringing the charge home against himself.

— Confucianism

Work to help everyone who is weak.

— New Testament

The wisdom of this world is foolish.

— New Testament